More to explore

On some of the pages in this book, you will find coloured buttons with symbols on them. There are four different colours, and each belongs to a different topic. Choose a topic, follow its coloured buttons through the book, and you'll make some interesting discoveries of your own.

For example, on page 6 you'll find an orange button like this, next to a picture of a racing car. The orange buttons are about engine power.

Page 15

Engine power

There is a page number in the button. Turn to that page (page 15) to find an orange button next to something else about engine power. Follow all the steps through the book, and at the end of your journey you'll find out how the steps are linked, and discover even more information about this topic.

Science

Safety first

People

The other topics in this book are science, safety first and people. Follow the steps and see what you can discover!

Machines on the move

Machines that help us to move from place to place are known as vehicles. Large vehicles, such as trains and ships, can move lots of people or goods in one go. Smaller vehicles, like motorcycles, may carry just one person at a time.

A cycle rickshaw carries schoolchildren through a city.

People ride in a cart attached to the bike.

Carts, sleds and wagons can be moved by animals. People around the world still use horses, donkeys, oxen and dogs to pull these machines along the ground.

Some vehicles are **powered by people**. On a bicycle, the rider pushes the pedals around with his or her feet and legs. The pedals turn a chain, which turns the back wheel around. This moves the bicycle forward.

A cyclist turns handlebars to steer the bicycle.

Handlebars turn the front wheel left or right.

chain

pedal

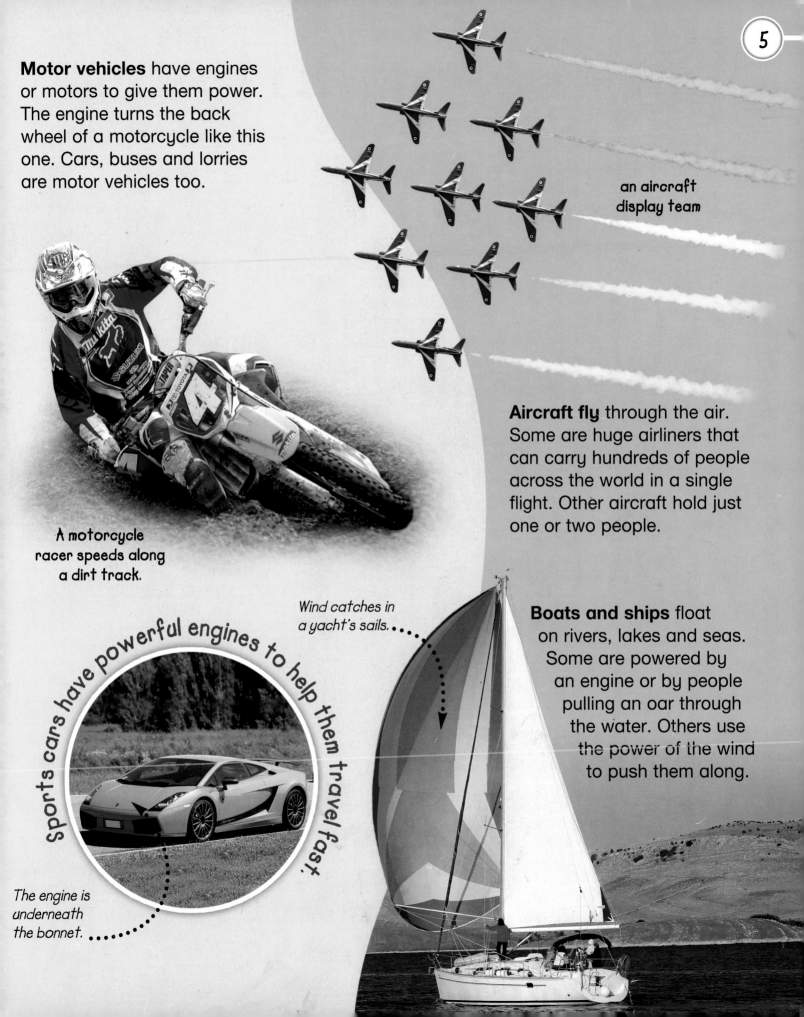

Motor vehicles have engines or motors to give them power. The engine turns the back wheel of a motorcycle like this one. Cars, buses and lorries are motor vehicles too.

an aircraft display team

A motorcycle racer speeds along a dirt track.

Aircraft fly through the air. Some are huge airliners that can carry hundreds of people across the world in a single flight. Other aircraft hold just one or two people.

Sports cars have powerful engines to help them travel fast.

Wind catches in a yacht's sails.

The engine is underneath the bonnet.

Boats and ships float on rivers, lakes and seas. Some are powered by an engine or by people pulling an oar through the water. Others use the power of the wind to push them along.

What is this?

1 crash barrier

2 Mechanics change a tyre in the pits.

3 A chequered flag signals the winner.

Page 27

Page 15

Daring racers

Ever since cars were invented, people have loved to race them. Today's Formula One racing cars are super-fast. They can reach up to 400 kilometres per hour – that's nearly four times the speed allowed on motorways! Thousands of fans gather to watch them race.

2

3

⚠️ Page 18

4

5

6

After 90 minutes of tough racing, car number 4 zooms across the finish line. It has won the race by less than a second! A Formula One race lasts 60–70 laps of the twisting, turning track. If a car has a problem, the driver can steer it off the track and into the pits. There his team will fix the car or fit new tyres – but they need to be quick!

↪ This is the steering wheel of a Formula One car.

How cars go

A car is powered by an engine. The engine
turns the car's wheels, driving the car forward.
A driver can speed up the car by pressing
a foot pedal called the accelerator.
Pressing the brake pedal will slow
the car down or stop it.

Mirrors help the driver to see what is behind the car.

The engine is under the bonnet.

Headlights light up the road ahead in the dark.

Hundreds of parts
make up a modern motor
car. The frame of the car is
called the chassis. Other big
parts, such as the engine,
doors and body panels,
are fixed to the chassis.

The radiator cools the engine down.

The steering wheel connects to the axle to turn the wheels.

A driver refuels his car at a pump.

Seatbelts keep people safely strapped in their seats.

Most car engines work by burning **fuel** such as petrol or diesel. This releases some harmful gases into the air. Some new cars have electric motors that run on battery power instead.

Gases from the engine come out of the exhaust pipe.

An electric car recharges its batteries.

Bumpers protect the front and back of a car.

Cars travel on road networks that link many different places.

Tyres help the wheels to grip on the road.

To start a car the driver turns the ignition key. This fires small sparks inside the engine and gets the car running. At the end of a journey, the driver turns the key again to stop the engine.

Roads are busy places, and drivers need to know how to use them safely. Signs warn drivers not to go over a certain speed. Signals such as traffic lights tell vehicles to stop to let other cars or people cross a road.

Transport in town

Every day, millions of people make journeys across towns and cities. Some people walk or cycle, while others drive in cars. Public transport vehicles, such as buses, trams and trains, move lots of people in one go. Traffic signals help to keep the roads and railways safe.

Page 30

What is this?

1. A bus stops to let people on or off.

2. A tram travels along a track.

3. monorail train

? A traffic light shines green. This tells vehicles that they can move ahead.

In this busy city, roads are not the only places for machines on the move. Above the streets, a monorail train cruises along a high track. Below the streets, subway trains carry people through underground tunnels. Both subway and monorail trains stop at station platforms where passengers can get on and off.

Page 27

4 traffic policeman
on a motorcycle

5 escalator to and from
the subway

6 Subway trains arrive
at a platform.

On track

Trains run on railway tracks from one place to another. Their wheels have a special shape that fits over the rails and keeps them on the track. At the front of a train is a locomotive engine. This can pull many carriages or wagons behind it.

Steam trains get their power from steam, which is made by heating water in a big boiler. The steam pushes parts of the steam engine, making it turn the wheels round.

Tracks are made of long rails and shorter sleepers.

rail   sleeper

This high-speed train is called a bullet train.

These people are inside a city subway train.

Steam puffs out of the train's chimney.

This freight train uses diesel to power its engine.

Bullet trains are powered by electric cables.

Up to 1,300 passengers can travel in the train's carriages.

Trains don't just carry people, they pull heavy loads too. **Freight trains** move materials such as sand or coal across the countryside. Some freight trains are very long as they are made up of 50 or more wagons.

The driver controls the train from the cab.

The fastest trains that carry passengers are called bullet trains. They were first built in Japan and can travel at over 275 kilometres per hour.

Underground trains travel through long tunnels below the ground, mostly in busy towns and cities. Some trains go through tunnels under the sea. Eurotunnel trains carry people, and even cars, under the sea between England and France.

1 cement mixer

2 A crane lifts heavy steel girders.

3 The girders arrived here on a truck.

What is this?

Heavyweight vehicles

People use huge vehicles to build things such as houses, offices, bridges and roads. Trucks carry materials to a building site. Fork lifts, cranes and tractor loaders move these materials around. Cranes lift loads up high and excavators reach low to dig big holes in the ground.

Page 18

5

6

Page 22

7

At this noisy building site, trucks deliver girders and bricks, while other vehicles move them around. A dump truck tips sand out of its trailer. Some of this will be taken to the cement mixer, where it will be churned with other materials to make cement.

This is a close-up of the tread on a truck's tyre, which helps it to grip the ground.

Hauling heavy loads

Some vehicles are built to carry really large or heavy things. These machines have to be very tough. They need big, powerful engines so that they can transport their load – which may be heavy firefighting equipment, or even a house!

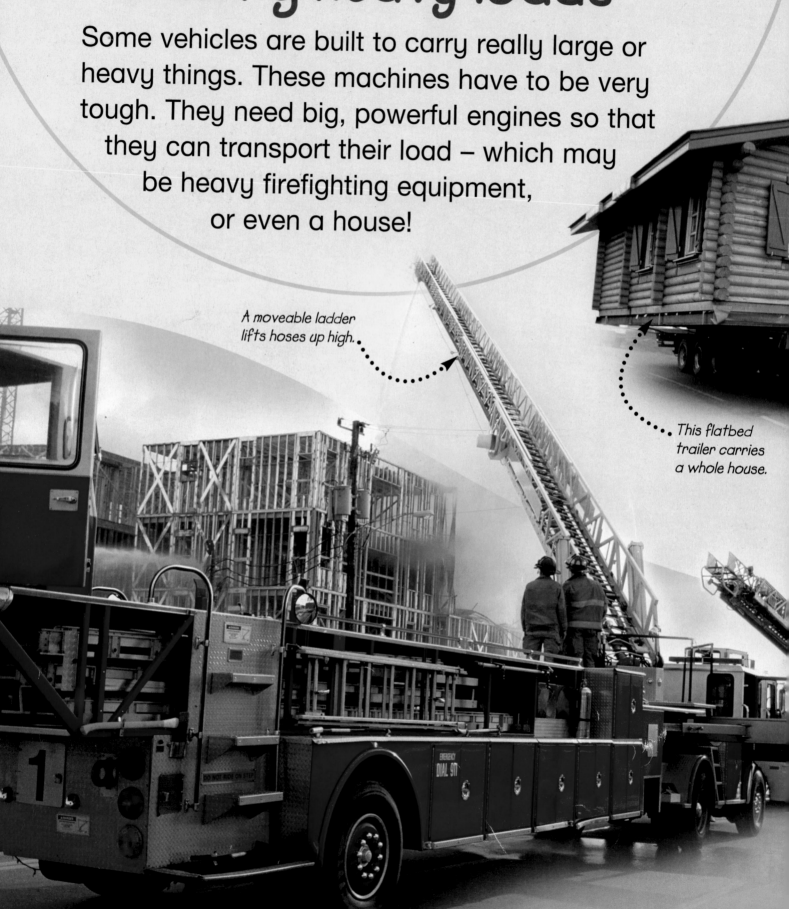

A moveable ladder lifts hoses up high.

This flatbed trailer carries a whole house.

Articulated trucks have a driver's cab that can be fixed to different trailers. Some trailers are box-shaped and can hold goods inside. Flatbed trailers are flat with no sides, so large loads can rest on top.

A road train travels through Australia.

Road trains have a powerful cab that can pull two, three or more trailers at once. They are used to transport things long distances, through areas with few towns.

Giant dump trucks are used in mining to move large loads of rock.

The engine is in the cab part, giving it power to pull the trailer.

The driver looks tiny next to these 3-metre wheels!

Fire engines carry water, ladders, pumps and other firefighting equipment quickly to a fire. Their ladders stretch upwards to reach fires or rescue people trapped in tall buildings.

Car transporters move cars from the factories where they were made to showrooms where they go on sale. This transporter carries ten cars, all fixed securely in place.

1 A ground marshal directs a plane.

2 wheels for take-off and landing

3 pilot in the cockpit

4 truck with trailer full of luggage

What is this?

Page 22

Page 26

High fliers

Aircraft fly all over the world, taking off and landing on flat, smooth strips called runways. Airports often have more than one runway so that several planes can take off and land at the same time. On the ground, other vehicles help to transport passengers and their luggage around.

Page 30

An aircraft speeds along the runway, takes off and flies into the air. Inside the cockpit, the pilot is in control. He must fly safely over land and sea, to another airport where the plane will land. Passengers from a larger aircraft are unloading in the background. They've arrived for their holidays! A staircase is wheeled over to let them off the plane.

This is a propeller. It spins round very fast and helps to power the plane through the sky.

Take-off

An aircraft starts its journey by moving faster and faster along the ground. Air flows over the aircraft's wings, which helps to lift it off the runway and up into the air. Giant jet engines give the plane power to speed along.

cockpit

In the cockpit, the pilot and co-pilot steer the aircraft and check that all of its parts are working. They use their controls to make the aircraft turn, climb higher or dive down.

Wheels rise up into the body of the plane after take-off.

jet engine

Jet engines thrust out hot gases, forcing the plane forward.

Hot air balloons are filled with air, which is heated by a burner. The warm air rises, carrying the balloon up into the sky.

Passengers ride in the basket.

A large airliner like this one needs lots of power to speed along the runway and rise into the air. This power comes from four huge jet engines, fixed underneath the wings.

A helicopter hovers to rescue a person in trouble.

Rotor blades spin to let the helicopter hover in mid-air.

Elevator flaps help the plane to fly up or down.

The body of a plane is called the fuselage.

Sea planes can take off from lakes, rivers and seas. Instead of wheels, they have large floats full of air. These allow the plane to rest on the surface of the water.

Riding the waves

Ships and boats travel the waters of the world. They take people on fun trips, and carry passengers and their cars across rivers and seas. Many ships move large amounts of goods, called cargo. They sail into ports or harbours where they can transfer their loads to or from the land.

2574

2

3

1

⚠️
Page 10

4

What is this?

① catamaran, a type of sailing boat

② fishing trawler

③ A tug boat tows larger boats in and out of harbour.

? This is a boat anchor. It is dropped to the bottom of the sea to hold the boat still.

ISABELLA

6

5

75632

Page 19

Page 30

This harbour is full of action, with boats cruising in and out from the sea. A family has fun on a speed boat, while other people are hard at work. Fishermen on a trawler haul in their nets. A huge container ship unloads its cargo. The coloured crates contain goods which will then travel on by truck or train.

4 A speed boat prepares to race away.

5 A coastguard boat checks everyone is safe on the water.

6 Cranes unload a giant container ship.

Floating and diving

Boats and ships float on top of the water. Their shape pushes away the water and keeps them above the surface. Boats come in many shapes and sizes, but they must be carefully made so that they don't tip over or sink.

This rubber boat is filled with air.

Boats float because they are lighter than the water they push away. Some materials, like wood, float naturally. Other materials can be made to float by filling them with air. Air is much lighter than water, so the boat can carry people and still not sink.

Paddling pushes the water back, which moves the boat forward.

Amphibious vehicles can travel on both land and water.

wheels for use on land

The body of a boat is called its **hull**. The boat's hull presses down on the water and the water pushes back. This keeps the boat afloat.

hull

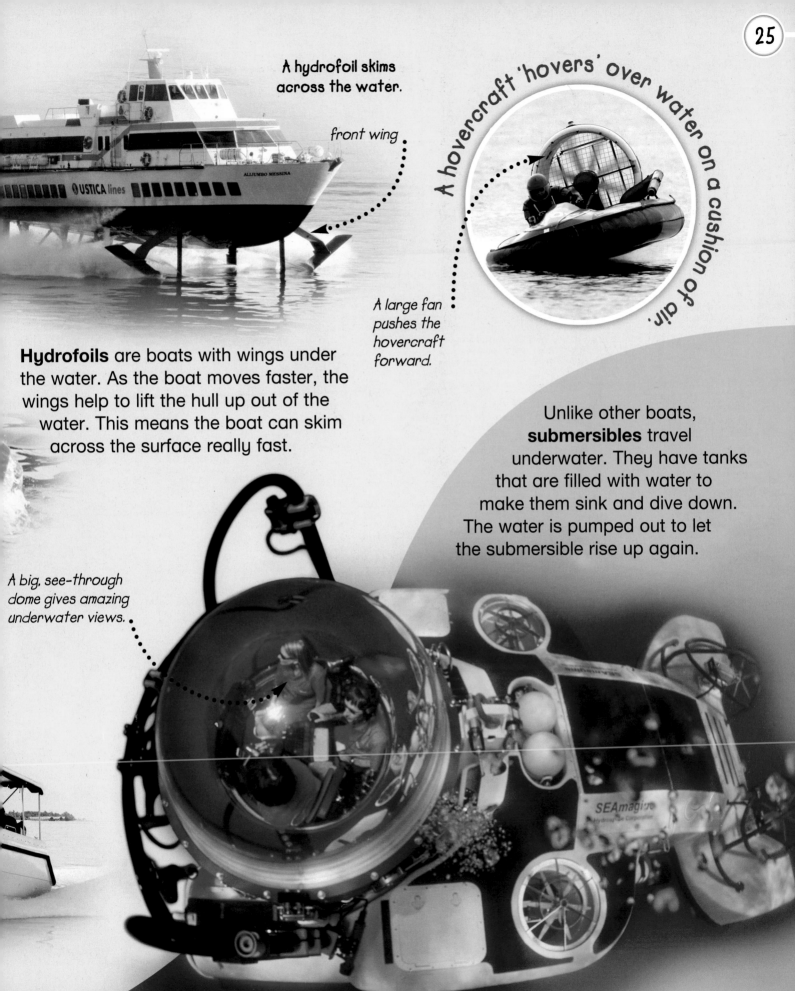

A hydrofoil skims across the water.

front wing

A hovercraft 'hovers' over water on a cushion of air.

A large fan pushes the hovercraft forward.

Hydrofoils are boats with wings under the water. As the boat moves faster, the wings help to lift the hull up out of the water. This means the boat can skim across the surface really fast.

Unlike other boats, **submersibles** travel underwater. They have tanks that are filled with water to make them sink and dive down. The water is pumped out to let the submersible rise up again.

A big, see-through dome gives amazing underwater views.

Really fast rockets

A space rocket blasts hot gases downwards to thrust itself up into the sky. The blast is enough to drive the rocket away from Earth and far off into space. Inside the rocket is its payload. This may be a satellite that takes pictures of Earth, or even astronauts on a space mission.

Page 30

What is this?

① This transporter carried the rocket to its launchpad.

② The launchpad is hidden by gases from the exhausts.

③ The main rocket is over 40 metres tall.

? This is a group of exhausts – tubes at the bottom of a rocket where the hot gases blast out.

Page 23

6

5

Page 15

Five... four... three... two... one... LIFT-OFF! A giant space rocket shoots into the air as its engines fire. Clouds of hot gas blast out of the exhaust tubes, lifting the rocket upwards. At first, the rocket rises slowly because of its great weight. It will soon start to build up speed so that it zooms into space very fast.

4 Booster rockets give launch power but fall away soon after lift-off.

5 This rocket carries a satellite as its payload.

6 space centre buildings

Record breakers

Some people try to build machines that go faster than any before. These record-breaking vehicles need really powerful engines. They need a smooth, sleek body to zoom through the air, water or space. They also need a brave driver!

Thrust SSC is the world's fastest machine on land. In 1997, it raced along a flat desert and reached an amazing speed of 1,228 kilometres per hour. It was powered by two jet engines, normally used in jet fighter planes.

The fastest racing cars are called Top Fuel dragsters. These cars race in pairs along a straight piece of track. They finish their 400 metre-long race in less than five seconds. Wow!

A TGV train in France once travelled at over 570 kilometres per hour.

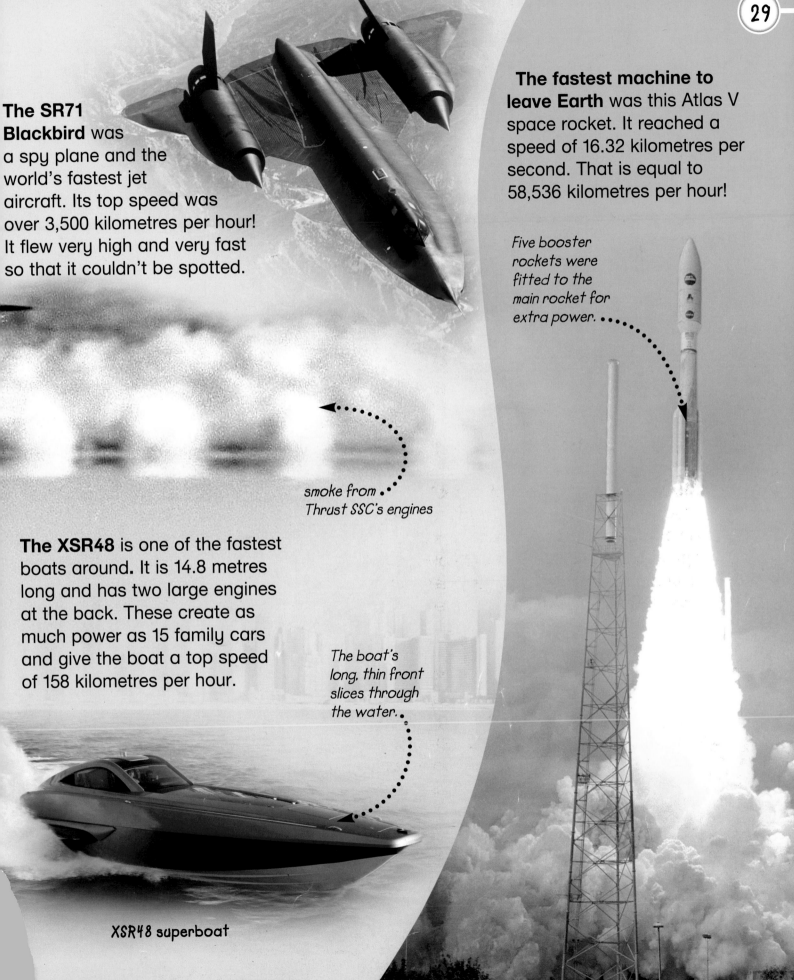

The SR71 Blackbird was a spy plane and the world's fastest jet aircraft. Its top speed was over 3,500 kilometres per hour! It flew very high and very fast so that it couldn't be spotted.

The fastest machine to leave Earth was this Atlas V space rocket. It reached a speed of 16.32 kilometres per second. That is equal to 58,536 kilometres per hour!

Five booster rockets were fitted to the main rocket for extra power.

smoke from Thrust SSC's engines

The XSR48 is one of the fastest boats around. It is 14.8 metres long and has two large engines at the back. These create as much power as 15 family cars and give the boat a top speed of 158 kilometres per hour.

The boat's long, thin front slices through the water.

XSR48 superboat

Engine power

A Formula One car engine is very powerful. It enables the car to **accelerate** (speed up) from sitting still to 200 kilometres per hour in less than 4 seconds!

The world's **largest dump trucks** are over 15 metres long and 7 metres tall. Their giant engines give them power to carry up to 360 tonnes of rock – that is heavier than 50 adult elephants!

Science

Racing vehicles have a smooth shape so that air flows easily around their body. This is called **streamlining**. It helps the vehicle to race forwards more quickly.

Rockets send space **satellites** high above Earth's surface. There, they travel in a big circle around the planet. Some satellites are used to bounce TV pictures or telephone calls from one part of the world to another.

Safety first

A **strong harness** straps a racing driver firmly into his seat. He wears a special suit that protects him against flames if there is a fire. A helmet protects his head.

Before a plane takes off, staff onboard carry out a **safety demonstration**. They show passengers how to fasten their seatbelts and what to do if there is a problem during the flight.

People

The driver of a bus, tram or train follows a set route and timetable to get passengers to the right place at the right time. He or she keeps in touch with station workers by radio, reporting any problems along the way.

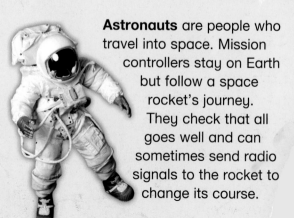

Astronauts are people who travel into space. Mission controllers stay on Earth but follow a space rocket's journey. They check that all goes well and can sometimes send radio signals to the rocket to change its course.

More to explore

Huge passenger airliners have four or more powerful jet engines. The biggest of all is the **Airbus A380**, which can carry up to 850 people. Its top speed is just over 1,000 kilometres per hour!

The engines of the **Saturn V space rocket** packed more power than 300,000 sports cars! Saturn V was as tall as a 36-floor building. From lift-off, it took just two-and-a-half minutes to climb 68 kilometres into the sky.

Caterpillar tracks are fitted to many heavy vehicles to stop them from sinking into soft or muddy ground. The tracks work by spreading the weight of the vehicle over a larger area than an ordinary wheel and tyre.

A **rudder** is a flat fin that is fitted to the back of a boat. It sits underwater and is used for steering. Pushing the rudder one way or the other changes the flow of water around the boat and helps it to turn.

Many people on boats wear **lifejackets**. These are either full of air or a very light material like foam, which floats well in water. Lifejackets help to stop people from sinking under the water if they fall in.

Cycle lanes are parts of roads that are marked off especially for bicycles. This separates the cyclists from the other traffic and helps to keep them safe. Cycle lanes are found in most big towns and cities.

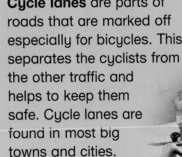

Coastguards try to keep everyone safe at sea. Sometimes they rush out of the harbour to help a boat or swimmer in trouble. At other times, they check on boat safety or help to fight crimes on the water.

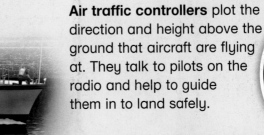

Air traffic controllers plot the direction and height above the ground that aircraft are flying at. They talk to pilots on the radio and help to guide them in to land safely.

Index